Summer

Fun under the Sun

TO:

FROM:

It is summer, let mind dances like the waves with the music of ocean breeze

Debasish Mridha, MD

"IT'S SUMMER AND TIME FOR WANDERING"

Kellie Elmore

"REJOICE AS SUMMER SHOULD...
CHASE AWAY SORROWS BY LIVING."

MELISSA MARR

O'NEILL
KAPOWUI
California
KAPOWUI
dmv.ca.gov
(800) 200.0003

"SUN IS SHINING.
WEATHER IS SWEET.
MAKE YOU WANNA MOVE YOUR DANCING FEET."

Bob Marley

"THE TANS WILL FADE BUT THE MEMORIES WILL LAST FOREVER."

Unknown

"IN SUMMER, THE SONG SINGS ITSELF."

WILLIAM CARLOS WILLIAMS

Architecte d'intérieur
Raj-Mahal Spécialités Inc

"THERE IS NO 'WE' IN SUMMER.
ONLY 'U' AND 'ME'."

Unknown

"SUMMERTIME IS ALWAYS THE
BEST OF WHAT MIGHT BE."

CHARLES BOWDEN

"LIVE IN THE SUNSHINE,
SWIM THE SEA,
DRINK THE WILD AIR."

Ralph Waldo Emerson

"LET US DANCE IN THE SUN,
WEARING WILD FLOWERS IN OUR HAIR"

SUSAN POLIS SCHUTZ

"IT'S A SMILE, IT'S A
KISS, IT'S A SIP OF WINE...
IT'S SUMMERTIME!"

KENNY CHESNEY

"SUMMER'S LEASE HATH ALL
TOO SHORT A DATE."

WILLIAM SHAKESPEARE

"THE END-OF-SUMMER WINDS MAKE PEOPLE RESTLESS."

SEBASTIAN FAULKS

"DEEP SUMMER IS WHEN LAZINESS FINDS RESPECTABILITY."

SAM KEEN

"IT'S A SURE SIGN OF SUMMER IF THE CHAIR GETS UP WHEN YOU DO."

WALTER WINCHELL

"SUMMER VACATION: WHERE YOU DRINK TRIPLE, SEE DOUBLE AND ACT SINGLE."

UNKNOWN

"BE SURE NOT TO FIZZLE WHEN THE SUMMER STARTS TO SIZZLE"

Unknown

"THOSE LAZY-HAZY-CRAZY DAYS OF SUMMER."

NAT KING COLE

"WHEN THE SUN IS SHINING I CAN DO ANYTHING; NO MOUNTAIN IS TOO HIGH, NO TROUBLE TOO DIFFICULT TO OVERCOME."

WILMA RUDOLPH

Life is like the ocean. It can be calm and still and rough or rigid. But in the end, it is always beautiful

Unknown